EVERYDAY SCIENCE

Magnets

Please visit our web site at: www.garethstevens.com
For a free color catalog describing Gareth Stevens Publishing's list of high-quality books
and multimedia programs, call 1-800-542-2595 or fax your request to (414) 332-3567.

Library of Congress Cataloging-In-Publication Data

Riley, Peter D.
    Magnets / by Peter Riley. — North American ed.
      p. cm. — (Everyday science)
    Summary: Describes different kinds of magnets and uses simple
experiments to explain how magnetism works.
    Includes bibliographical references and index.
    ISBN 0-8368-3250-7 (lib. bdg.)
    1. Magnets—Juvenile literature.   2. Magnetism—Juvenile literature.
[1. Magnets—Experiments.   2. Magnetism—Experiments.   3. Experiments.]
I. Title.
QC757.5.R55   2002
538.4—dc21   2002022636

This North American edition first published in 2002 by
Gareth Stevens Publishing
A World Almanac Education Group Company
330 West Olive Street, Suite 100
Milwaukee, Wisconsin 53212 USA

Original text © 2001 by Peter Riley. Images © 2001 by Franklin Watts.
First published in 2001 by Franklin Watts, 96 Leonard Street, London, EC2A 4XD, England.
This U.S. edition © 2002 by Gareth Stevens, Inc.

Series Editor: Rachel Cooke
Designers: Jason Anscomb, Michael Leamen Design Partnership
Photography: Ray Moller (unless otherwise credited)
Gareth Stevens Editor: Lizz Baldwin

Picture Credit: Rex Features, p. 15.

The original publisher thanks the following children for modeling for this book: Jordan Conn, Nicola Freeman, Charley Gibbens,
Alex Jordan, Eddie Lengthorn, and Rachael Moodley.

Printed in Hong Kong

1 2 3 4 5 6 7 8 9 06 05 04 03 02

Magnets

Written by Peter Riley

Gareth Stevens Publishing
A WORLD ALMANAC EDUCATION GROUP COMPANY

About This Book

Everyday Science is designed to encourage children to think about their everyday world in a scientific way, by examining cause and effect through close observation and discussing what they have seen. Here are some tips to help you get the most from **Magnets**.

• This book introduces the basic concepts of magnets and some of the vocabulary associated with them, such as the comparison of strong and stronger, and it prepares children for more advanced learning about magnets.

• On pages 11, 17, and 23, children are asked to predict the results of a particular action or test. Be sure to discuss the reasons for any answers they give before turning the page. The questions on pages 11 and 17 each have only one correct answer. Discuss reasons for each correct answer, then set up other tests for the children and discuss possible outcomes.

• You can link the study of magnets with other areas of science, such as materials and their properties (pages 8 to 13) or forces and movement (pages 14 to 27).

• The images in this book can be used as a guide for showing the results of magnetic tests. Encourage children to put directional arrows on their own diagrams, as we have done on page 17. These arrows show children that a force works in a particular direction.

• The question on page 16 can lead to further discussion of Earth's magnetic force. The swinging magnet test on pages 18 and 19 can easily be adapted to learning how to use a simple compass.

Contents

Where is the best place to find magnets at home?

In the kitchen! Magnets hold things on a refrigerator door. Strip magnets inside the refrigerator door help it stay closed tightly.

The magnets used in science experiments come in many different shapes and sizes.

Some magnets are shaped like horseshoes.

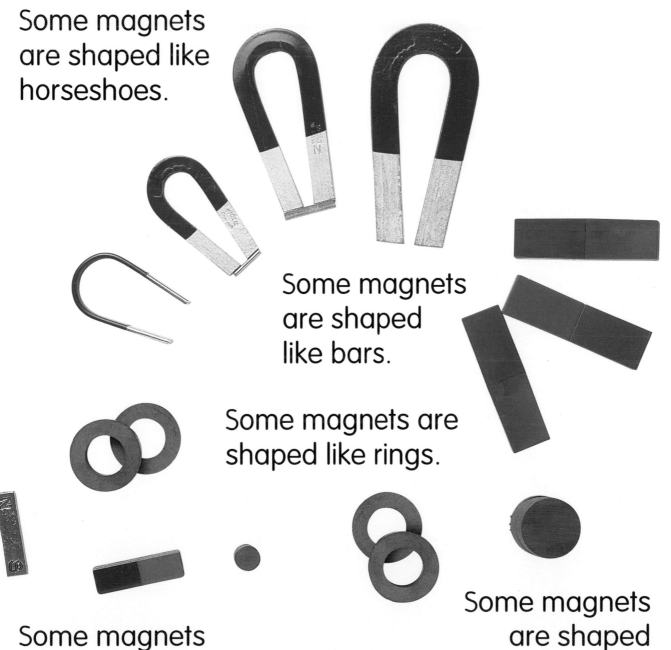

Some magnets are shaped like bars.

Some magnets are shaped like rings.

Some magnets are flat.

Some magnets are shaped like disks.

Magnetic Materials

A magnet sticks to steel.

A magnet sticks to iron.

Steel and iron are called magnetic materials because they stick to a magnet.

8

A magnet does not stick to these materials.

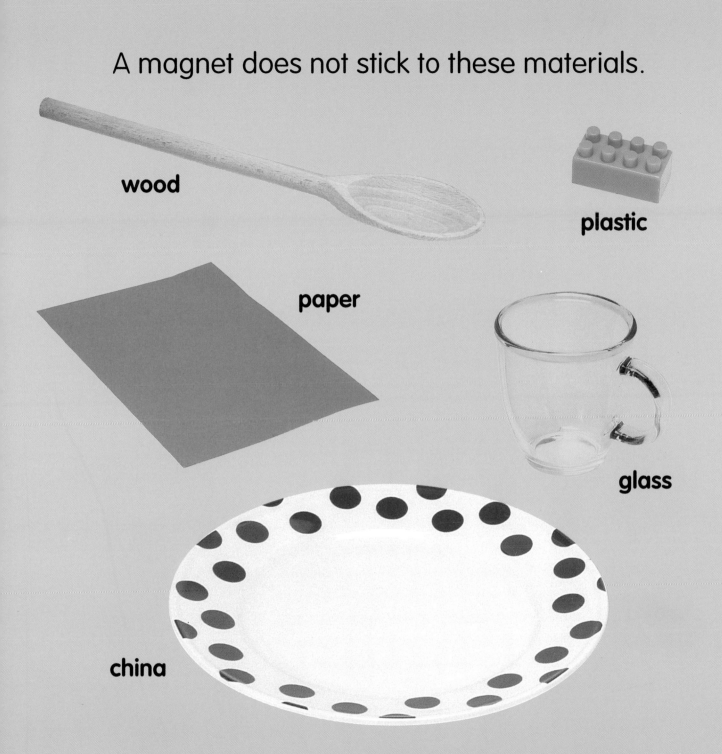

wood

plastic

paper

glass

china

Materials that do not stick to a magnet
are called non-magnetic materials.

9

Magnetic Test

Adam has some objects made of different materials. He wants to find out which of the objects are magnetic.

copper scouring pad

brass doorknob

iron pan

ceramic mug

plastic car

aluminum foil

steel bowl

He tests each object with a magnet.

He puts the magnet on the material.

The magnet sticks to magnetic materials.

The magnet does not stick to non-magnetic materials.

What will the results of Adam's tests be?
Turn the page to find out.

Test Results

The magnet sticks to the iron pan and the steel bowl.

The magnet does not stick to the aluminum foil, the ceramic mug, the brass doorknob, the plastic car, or the copper scouring pad.

Iron, steel, aluminum, brass,
and copper are all metals.

Adam's tests show that
iron and steel are magnetic.

They also show that brass, copper,
and aluminum are non-magnetic.

What do Adam's tests tell us about metals?

Magnetic Force

Bring a
magnet
close to a
steel spoon.

The magnet
pulls the spoon.

This pull is called
magnetic force.

Magnetic force makes the
spoon move toward the
magnet and stick to it.

To take the spoon away from the magnet, you have to pull them apart.

Your pulling force must be stronger than the magnetic force.

Some large magnets have a very strong magnetic force. They can lift huge pieces of metal.

What can large magnets be used for?

Magnets Have **Poles**

The ends of this bar magnet are called poles.

The red end is the south pole.

The blue end is the north pole.

Both ends attract magnetic materials.

Earth has a north pole and a south pole. Where are they?

When two south poles are held
near each other, they push apart.

When a south pole and a north pole are held
near each other, they pull together.

What happens when two north poles
are held near each other?
Turn the page to find out.

17

The Magnet  Swings!

When two north poles are held near each other, the magnets push each other away.

Claire has tied a string around a bar magnet. She holds onto the string and keeps the magnet steady. Then she brings the south pole of another bar magnet close to the south pole of the magnet on the string.

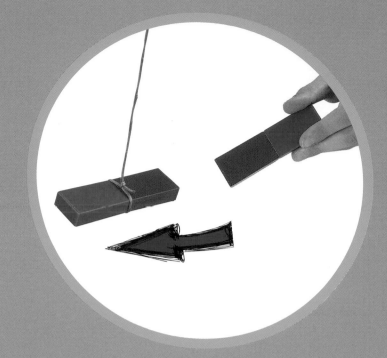

The magnet on the string swings **away** from the bar magnet Claire is holding.

When Claire brings the south pole of the other bar magnet close to the north pole of the magnet on the string, the magnet on the string swings **toward** the bar magnet she is holding.

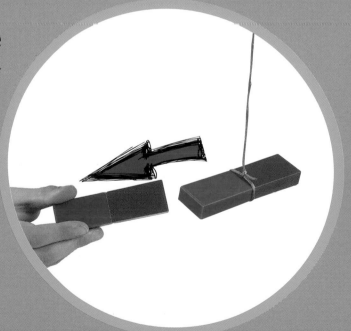

What happens when Claire brings the north poles of both magnets close to each other?

A Horseshoe Magnet

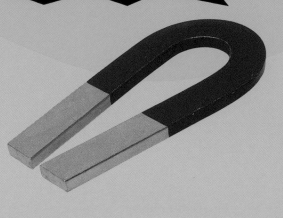

A horseshoe magnet has a north pole and a south pole, but the poles are not marked blue or red.

Natasha uses a bar magnet to find out which pole of the horseshoe magnet is north and which pole is south.

She brings the north pole of the bar magnet close to one pole of the horseshoe magnet.

The horseshoe magnet pushes away. This pole on the horseshoe magnet is the north pole.

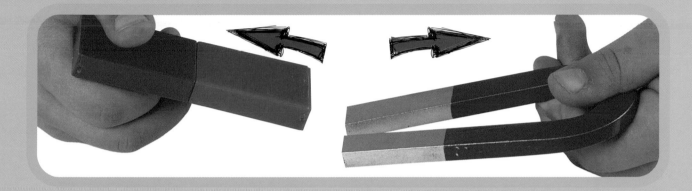

Natasha brings the north pole of the bar magnet close to the other pole of the horseshoe magnet.

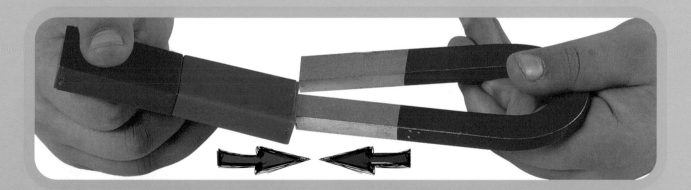

The two magnets stick together. This pole on the horseshoe magnet is the south pole.

Test the Force

1. Put a piece of cardboard over a steel screw.

2. Put one end of a magnet on top of the cardboard.

3. Lift the magnet.

4. The screw is stuck to the magnet. The cardboard is stuck between them.

5. Put two pieces of cardboard between the magnet and the screw.

6. The screw still sticks to the magnet, even through two pieces of cardboard.

7. Try this test with three pieces of cardboard. What do you think will happen? Turn the page to find out.

Magnetic  Strength

The screw does not stick to the magnet.

The pieces of cardboard do not stick between the screw and the magnet.

Three pieces of cardboard are too thick. The magnetic force is not strong enough to make the screw stick to the magnet through three pieces of cardboard.

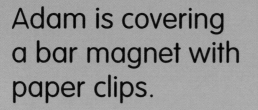

Adam is covering
a bar magnet with
paper clips.

He picks up the
bar magnet. The
paper clips stick
only to the poles
of the magnet.

The magnetic force is strongest at the poles.
Where would the paper clips stick if you covered
a horseshoe magnet with them?

Which Is **Strongest?**

Nadia wants to see which of her magnets has the strongest magnetic force.

She puts a paper clip at the starting end of a ruler.

She slides a bar magnet slowly alongside the ruler toward the paper clip.

At the place where the magnetic force starts to pull the paper clip toward the magnet, she measures the space between the paper clip and the magnet.

Nadia writes down her test results in a table.

Type of Magnet	Pole	Inches	(mm)
bar	N	$1\frac{1}{10}$	(28)
	S	1	(25)
disk	N	$\frac{8}{10}$	(20)
	S	$\frac{8}{10}$	(20)
horseshoe	N	1	(25)
	S	$\frac{9}{10}$	(23)
ring	N	$\frac{6}{10}$	(15)
	S	$\frac{6}{10}$	(15)
flat	N	$\frac{2}{10}$	(5)
	S	$\frac{2}{10}$	(5)

Try Nadia's test with your magnets.

Useful Words

attract: to bring something closer by means of an unseen force, such as magnetic force.

experiment: a carefully done test to find out whether or not an idea, or theory, is correct.

force: a push or a pull that makes something move, stop moving, or change its direction or its shape.

magnet: an iron or steel object that can pull magnetic materials toward it.

magnetic force: the push or pull created by a magnet.

magnetic materials: materials that will stick to a magnet.

materials: the many different kinds of matter that objects are made of, such as plastic, wood, and metal.

metals: materials such as iron, copper, and aluminum, which are usually shiny and can hold heat and electricity.

non-magnetic materials: materials that will not stick to a magnet.

poles: the north and south ends of a magnet, where the magnetic force is the strongest.

Some Answers

Here are some answers to the questions asked in this book. If you had different answers, you may be right, too. Talk over your answers with other people and see if you can explain why they are right.

page 13   Adam's tests tell us that not all metals are magnetic. Some metals are non-magnetic.

page 15   Large magnets are used in junkyards to pick up and move metal objects. They are also used to sort different types of metal garbage, such as steel and aluminum cans, so the metals can be recycled.

page 16   Earth's north and south poles are places at the top and the bottom of the planet, where it is very cold all year long. The north pole is in the Arctic, and the south pole is in the Antarctic. They are called poles because Earth is, in fact, a giant, ball-shaped magnet!

page 19   When Claire brings the north poles of both magnets close to each other, the magnet on the string will swing away from the other magnet, just as it did when she brought the two south poles close to each other.

page 25   On a horseshoe magnet, paper clips would stick to the north and south poles at the open end of the horseshoe shape.

For More Information

More Books to Read

- *Magnets. Simply Science* (series)
  Darlene R. Stille
  (Compass Point Books)

- *Science Factory: Magnetism & Magnets*
  Michael Flaherty
  (Copper Beech Books)

- *What Makes a Magnet?*
  Franklyn M. Branley
  (Harper Trophy)

Web Sites

- BrainPOP: Motion & Forces
  www.brainpop.com/science/forces/magnetism

- Look Learn & Do: Build a Compass
  *www.looklearnanddo.com/documents/
  projects_compass.html*

Index